AF428739

This book
belongs to:

____

____

____

____

First published 2023 with an exclusive licence from the authors to CHEETAH® Purrrrrrr Publishing, an imprint of CHEETAH® Toys & More, LLC (CHEETAH®).

Contact us: 1-860-781-1276, 1-876-909-6311 (WhatsApp), info@mycheetahacademy.com; paulettetrowers@yahoo.com

ISBN 13: 979-8-3303-2997-7
ISBN 10: 8-3303-2997-7

Dear CHEETAH® family:

Our little books were specially created to help our early readers master their decoding skills and build reading fluency. The repetitive use of high-frequency words, word families, decodable words, rhymes, and vivid illustrations facilitates this process. Our stories complement the objectives and content highlighted in the Jamaica Early Childhood Curriculum Guide and the Ministry of Education and Youth Grade 1 National Standards Curriculum.

In journeying through our series, our little ones will develop a deeper awareness of and appreciation for our Jamaican culture. Our books also have universal appeal, as any early reader can identify with the characters, events and subjects in our texts. Readers will get to enjoy the stories, build vocabulary, and exercise critical thinking by engaging in the activities at the end of each story.

Additionally, as a precursor to our series, or as a support to it, we've created a decodable 'sentence strip' book for the very young readers and those who require more scaffolding. Happy reading!

CHEETAH®

Chasing and capturing your dreams with you.

C-DER™
CHEETAH Decodable & Early Readers
Exploring the alphabet is like setting out on a treasure hunt to discover hidden words. Let's go! Let's embark on a treasure hunt for words!

My decodable words:

fun, glad, can, clap, feet, tell, well, less, mess, get, yet, bib, crib, him, Jim, fit, bit, mitt, sit, stop, top, lot, not

Letter sounds:

- consonant sounds /t/, /b/, /f/, /m/ in the initial, medial and final positions in words

- short vowel sound /i/ in the initial and medial positions in words

Word families: 'ad', 'an', 'ap', 'ell', 'ess', 'et', 'ib', 'im', 'it', 'op', 'ot'

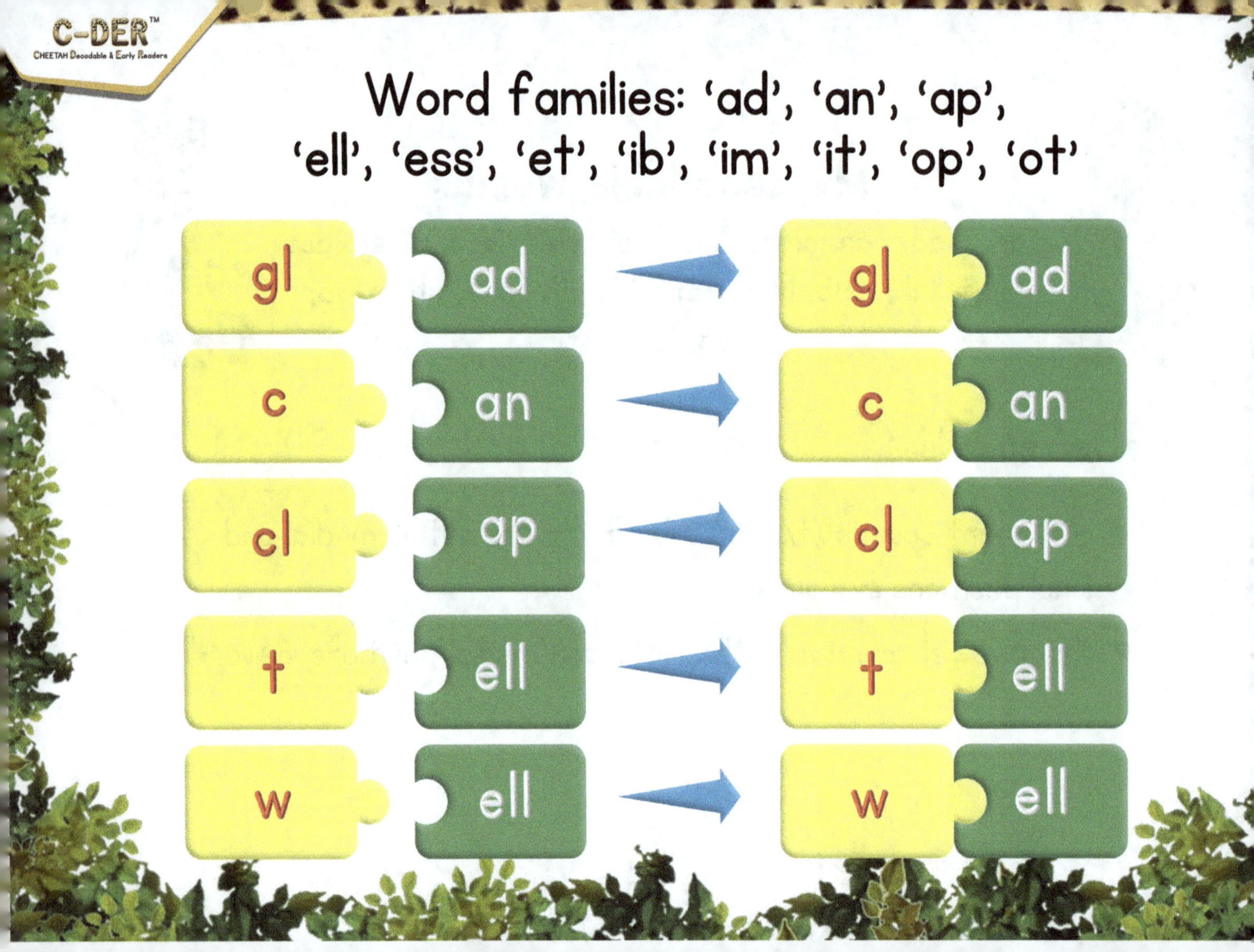

l ess
m ess
g et
y et
s it
l ess
m ess
g et
y et
s it
C-DER
CHEETAH Decodable & Early Readers

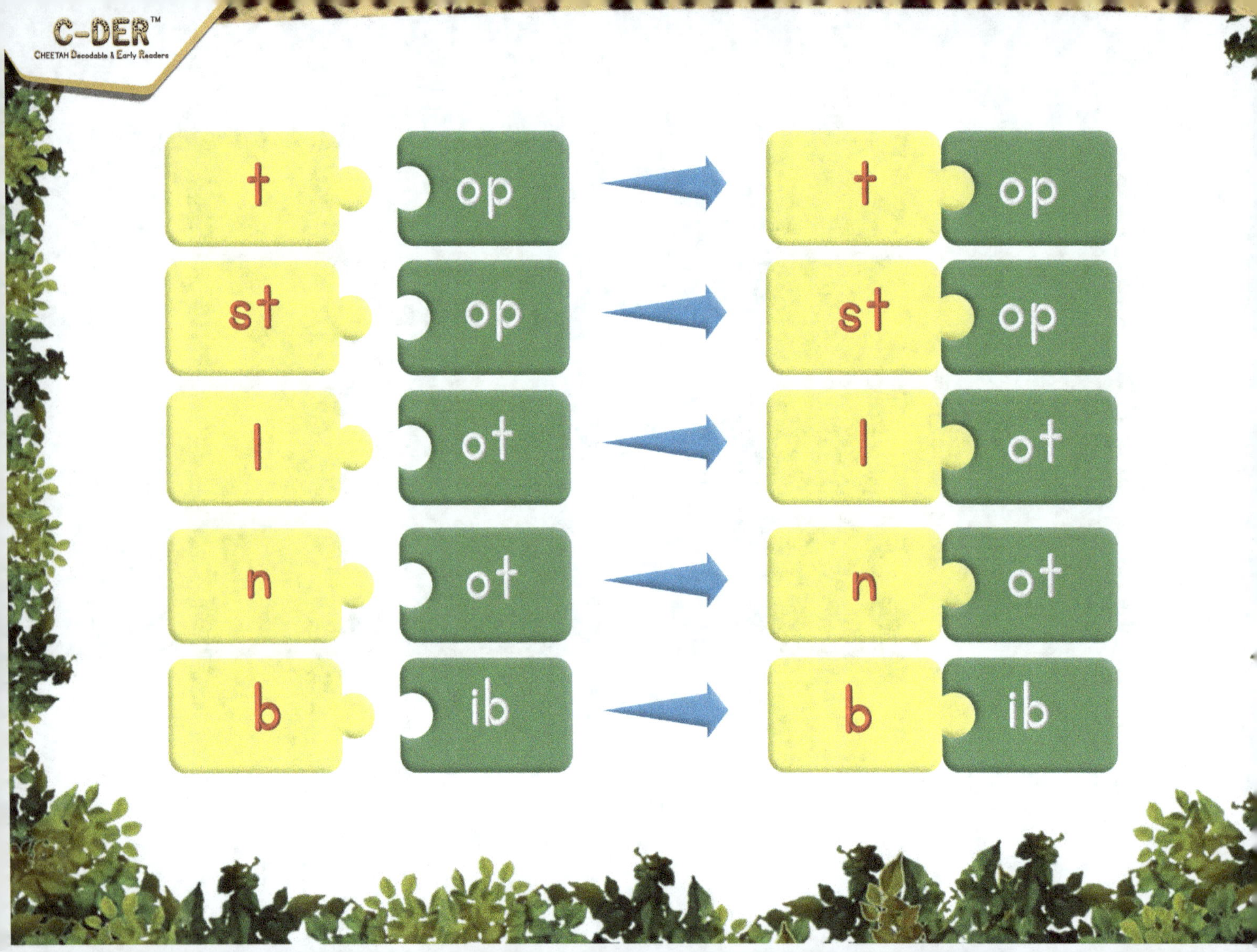

C-DER
CHEETAH Decodable & Early Readers
t | op
st | op
l | ot
n | ot
b | ib

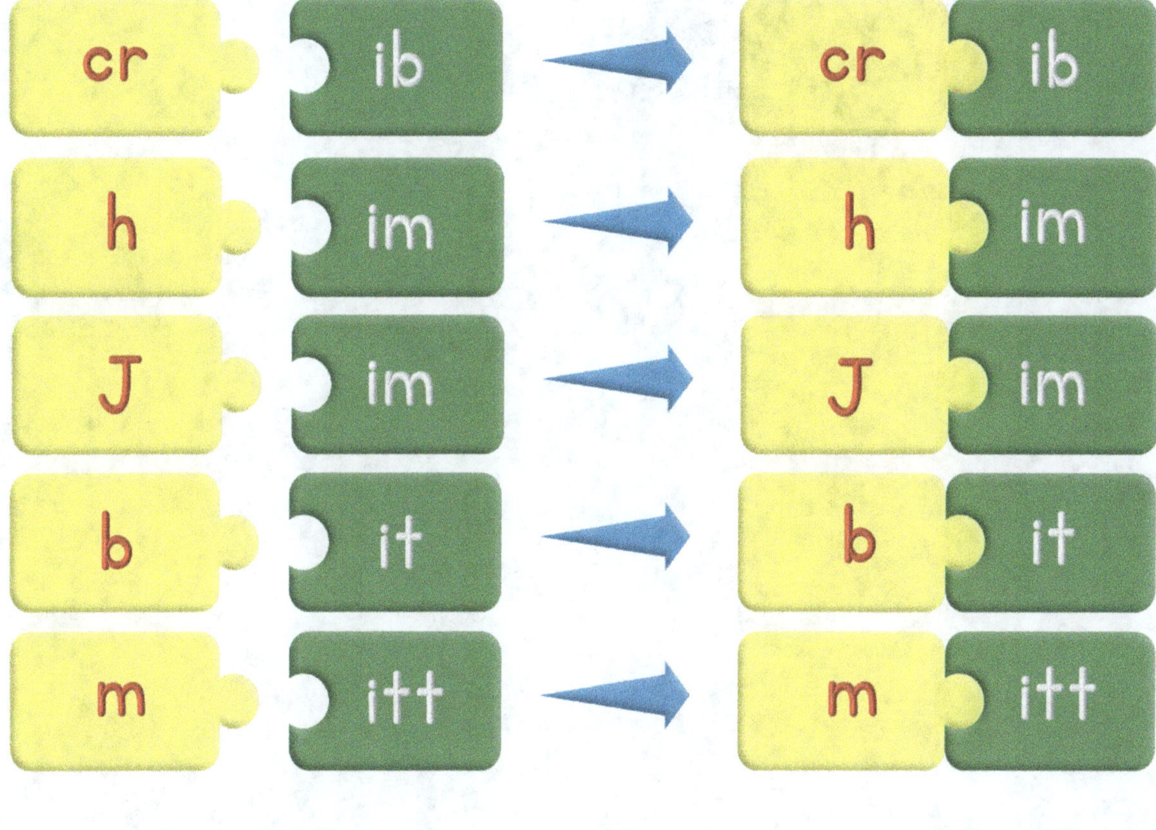
cr ib → cr ib
h im → h im
J im → J im
b it → b it
m itt → m itt

C-DER
CHEETAH Decodable & Early Readers
1

My Brother Jim

Look at him. He is my brother, Jim.

I love to sit and look at him.

He mostly stays inside his crib,

and almost always wears a bib.

C-DER
CHEETAH Decodable & Early Readers
3

He drinks his milk in little bits.

He does not like to wear his mitts.

His feet are so small that his socks do not fit,

and he lies in his crib like he cannot yet sit.

C-DER
CHEETAH Decodable & Early Readers
5

Jim likes to cry. I am not sure why.

It is hard to get him to stop, but I try.

I clap and make a funny face for Jim,

or I put on the music just for him.

C-DER
CHEETAH Decodable & Early Readers
7

I tell Mom, 'Jim can dance, you know.'

She says, 'Oh no. I do not think so.'

Jim moves a lot when the music plays.

I just love to watch him. I can watch him for days.

C-DER
CHEETAH Decodable & Early Readers
9

You must see what Jim does when his toy top spins.

His eyes open wide and he grins and grins.

He loves it when I play 'peek-a-boo'.

He looks at me and he starts to coo.

The other day, when Jim was sick,

we took him to see Doctor Nick.

He said, 'Jim's tooth is growing out.

There is nothing to worry about.'

C-DER™
CHEETAH Decodable & Early Readers
12

C-DER
CHEETAH Decodable & Early Readers
13

I am happy that Jim is now well.

As far as I can tell,

he is happy that he is well too,

so that he can do what he loves to do.

C-DER™
CHEETAH Decodable & Early Readers

I love Jim, and he loves me.

I am glad he is part of my family.

Even when he makes a mess,

I do not love him any less.

Discussion and activities:

1. Have the children talk about their younger or older siblings or cousins. Have them talk about the things that they like to do with them.

2. Have the children identify the words with the target letters and sounds.

3. Have the children make the sounds of the target letters and identify rhyming words in the text.

Discussion and activities:

4. Discuss the sound of the letters 'f' and 'oo' in the words 'fit' and 'coo' as used in the context of the story.

5. Have the children read the text aloud.

1. Why do you think Jim cries?

....

2. What are the things that Jim enjoys doing in the story?

....